KEEP WALKING IN PRAYER...

Until you can't come back

By Rev. Dorothy Scott Boulware

Dedication

*T*his book is dedicated to all the people who made the way of the Lord easy for me; who went through the gates, cast up the highway, gathered out the stones and prepared a way for this daughter of Zion.

To each of those people who made me know there was a place in the family of God for me, room at His feet, and that His greatest desire is for me to be in vital and lively relationship with Him. Bless the souls of those who have blessed me immensely, many of whose names are listed in the addendum.

It is also dedicated to those who have shared my journey up close and personal; my husband of 47 years, Oscar; my children: Toni Boulware and her husband Sam Stackhouse, Adrian Franklin, Paula Boulware and her husband Jamal Brown, Wanda Tere Boulware and James Pierce.

To my granddaughters Trenae Pitts and her husband Arlen Watson, Janiyah and Jasmine Brown, Jourdyn and Jaime Pierce. And my great grandson Arlen Watson Jr.

To my mother Magruder Cockrell, who is dancing in glory; to my grandmother Susan F. Fuller, who's directing a junior choir in heaven.

To my sister Charmaine Dixon and my sister Paula DeGraffinried, who is kicking cancer's butt!

I can never forget my oldest and dearest friends Bettie Crest Durant, Roslyn Horn Chester and Evon Taborn. Or my long time road buddy Rev. Robbin Blackwell or my newer spiritual sisters Rev. Bertha Borum and Rev. Lenora Howze.

As pastor, my chief ministers and intercessors, Rev. Felecia Diggs and Rev. Andre Newsome. And Apostle Stanley M. Butler who honored me by ordaining me because the Lord said so.

Introduction

I'm very happy with my prayer life. I'm exceedingly happy with my prayer life.

Yes, I said that to get your attention because no one ever says that.

I don't talk a lot about what goes on in my prayer time. Much of it is too wonderful to be spoken; it feels like mere words would somehow diminish the experience. Much of it is too high for me to understand so words wouldn't work anyway. But it gives life to my life, spring to my step, peace to my soul.

There is absolutely nothing like being in the presence of the Lord.

This is a point we sometimes miss while we bemoan our prayer inadequacies.

We're always moaning about not being "prayed up" whatever that is, about not praying long enough or not hearing from the Lord.

Seems as if our success driven society demands the same type of quantifiable markers from our prayer lives that are required in our professional endeavors. So we equate the shortage of marks on our prayer belts to our lack of stamina, inability to speak in more than one language, God's preference for people who have better prayer scores; or our final salvo…must not have been His will.

The premise of this book is simply that prayer is the ongoing transaction between us and the Lord and that can only be qualified or quantified by its very existence. Discipline is certainly an enhancement of the relationship as in any relationship, but who demands of us that we pray for hours on end on our knees or our faces, that we speak in tongues, that we fast until we're wan from the process. Or dictates that such stringent behavior will improve our outcomes.

Our parents used to say prayer is the soul's sincere desire. Prayer can be a word or a thought; a moan or a groan. A song. A sigh. Prayer can happen through what we wear–a piece of jewelry can be a reminder of a prayer concern. Prayer can happen with no action required beyond breathing.

Prayer is the ongoing transaction between us and God, mediated or spurred on by the Holy Spirit, with Jesus at the right hand of the Father interceding on our behalf. The Holy Spirit is the cutter. He makes sure the ball gets into the basket. Jesus is our elder brother who puts his seal of approval on us.

Satisfaction should come from the richness of the relationship, the fact that we share time and interchange thought, the fact that I can bask in His presence and He can complete whatever work He desires in and through me. Or just maybe make me smile from deep down in my soul as He assures me I'm His daughter.

During this time I acknowledge His grace of which I am a joyous recipient; celebrate His greatness, submit to His majesty, surrender my will, accept my call for the season or for the day. And there's no perfect time of day except the time we spend together. And there's no perfect length of time except that it should be difficult to turn my attention away. And there's no perfect way to spend the time except whatever He ordains for those moments.

And we are right to be daunted by the whole process of prayer with its mystery and its majesty. Experiments conducted years ago on the power of prayer reveal that even when doctors and patients were unaware that they were being prayed for, patients experienced more successful outcomes than those in the control group who were not being prayed for. Prayer accomplishes feats our minds can't even imagine; can't even fathom although we ask for them. People we pray for with the expectation that they live, die. People we pray for with submission to their transition, live.

And in the midst of life's contradictions, we continue to wonder why bad things happen to good people and vice versa. We continue to wonder why babies are born only to die very quickly. So many of our questions go unanswered regardless of our prayer. We're mere humans and God's ways are not our ways. And often we attribute to God's hand those things our own evil rebellion hath wrought through systems that perpetuate injustice and cruelty without measure.

I believe if we can think of prayer as relationship trans-action rather than requests submitted, answers received, yes or no; if we can embrace that prayer begins with the Lord and pulls us in, then we can relax and let Him do His thing.

By way of introduction, I'm a Baptist Methodist Pentecostal Evangelical non denominational retired pastor, retired newspaper editor, former minister of music, former fingerprint technician, wife of 47 years, mother of four, grandmother of five, great grandmother of one.

I began reading the Bible at four and soon after preached my first sermon at home. "How can you say you love God who you haven't seen and hate your brother who you see every day. You're a liar and the truth ain't in you." That was the whole sermon and that's enough of me for now.

In this book we'll embrace the reality of our relationship, acknowledging that God always hears us when we pray. I'll share prayer stories with you to encourage you and some-times to make you laugh. I'll introduce you to Mother Irene Montgomery who was the founding pastor of Prayer House of Our Father. My neighbor Sister Doris Payton invited me to her church for prayer and Bible study and was appalled when I came out of the house without a blanket. In Mother Montgomery's church, when you prayed, you cried; you cried out to the Lord and you postured yourself on a blanket either on your knees or your face. This was always done with full assurance that God would heed every call.

I'll tell you about the time I broke a promise to my youngest daughter based on nothing more than a feeling in my belly. I cancelled her going on a trip for no logical reason. The travelers were in a car accident. No one was seriously hurt. But maybe the position of passengers if increased by one might have made a difference in the outcome. Nothing like looking and feeling like a fool when you break a promise with the only explanation being "I don't know why," especially to a young teen.

Let's clarify. I don't want you to think I've cracked some kind of code or have some inroad unavailable to anyone else. Our God is no respecter of persons and eagerly welcomes us all. I am the proverbial "one beggar telling other beggars where I've found food." I've encountered so many friends, acquaintances and family members who feel unable to access God. They approach with fatalistic expectations of prayers never being answered, for whatever reasons — excess sin, ineffective methods, bad connection. Or they feel God will answer their prayers for other people but not for themselves.

This grieves my heart. There's not much more precious than the feeling of being heard. I could never have made it without knowing God has my back and I have God's ear. And I want everyone who wants it to have a similar expectation. I'm in a sweet spot on the journey and understand the journey is the prize rather than episodic outcomes that match my will. That's all.

I believe we can thrive in our prayer lives if we understand that God is always waiting to hear from us, to spend time with us. Yes, God is so much more than we can imagine, so much more than we are, and yet we mere mortals are eternally invited to fellowship in His presence.

If we understand that He delights in us and that's why the scripture encourages us to delight ourselves also in Him.

Please be kind enough to accompany me on a journey that will help us all reclaim our rightful places in the family of God...as heirs of God and joint heirs with Jesus Christ, with ministering angels who are sent forth to minister on our behalf daily.

Table of Contents

Prologue

I like equating prayer to walking because it's an ongoing action that's rhythmic and progressive. And it's something I can do easily and without help or props, even when I don't feel like it. I can choose to move when nothing in me agrees.

The prayer-walking biblical character who speaks volumes to me, although not very much in the bible, is Enoch. This is one of the shortest pieces in the bible.

Enoch was an ancestor of Noah, the son of Baraka and Jared. He was the father of Methuselah and Barakil. We know Methuselah because of bible trivia and colloquial usage. Who lived the longest in the bible? Methuselah, who lived 782 years. Or, "She's older than Methuselah."

While Enoch is the subject of many other writings, the bible simply records:

So all the days of Enoch were three hundred and sixty-five years. And Enoch walked with God: and he was not; for God took him. [Genesis 5:23,24]

Not much to that story, but I love it.

Enoch walked with God and he was not. I'm telling you, this is a preacher's delight. Just enough of a sermon tease to allow for Holy Ghost interpretation. I've written lessons and sermons on these tiny verses.

My take is that every day, Enoch walked with God. And he talked a lot and he listened a little.

And the next day, Enoch walked with God. And he talked a lot and he listened a little.

And the next day, Enoch walked with God. And he talked a lot and he listened a little.

And as the days progressed, as the years grew longer, Enoch walked with God and Enoch talked less and listened more. And less and less he talked. And more and more he listened.

And the family members began to say, "Do you think Enoch is acting strangely? He's so quiet most of the time. He doesn't argue like he used to. He doesn't cuss nearly as much. He even did me a favor the other day without my asking."

And the village people began to ask, "Have you seen Enoch lately? I don't see him as much as I used to. He used to come to the village gate and hang out with us men. But not so much lately. And the last time I saw him he seemed to have some kind of strange light on his face. I don't know what it was. But he's really different."

And even Enoch himself began to realize that things that used to bug him, didn't anymore. He realized that his temper had gotten so temperate that he hardly ever blew up anymore. He noticed that he longed for peace and quiet rather than the constant chatter of the children and grandchildren and great grand children of his family.

And every day Enoch would walk with God. And they became, as all friends eventually do, of one mind and one heart. Enoch finished God's sentences. And most of the time they didn't even have to talk because each one knew what the other was thinking.

It must have been a wonderful journey. It lasted 365 years – 365 years of walking and talking and walking and listening.

And every day Enoch would walk with God.

And one day, they looked at each other and decided their walking was complete, their talking was almost unnecessary and there was no real reason for them to part anymore.

And Enoch was not. God took him.

I could just jump into my testimony about how much I want this relationship and how much I want one day for God and myself to agree that there's no longer a need for our separation of any kind. One day I want my people to look for me and understand that I have, in an instant, become absent from the body to be present forever with my Lord.

Keep walking in prayer until you can't come back. Keep walking in prayer until you don't want to come back. Keep walking in prayer until the Lord is all you can see.

Can somebody say, "Hallelujah??!!!!"

CHAPTER 1.

God Always Hears Me When I Pray

I'm so grateful that God always hears me when I pray. Literally God hears me and lets me know I've been heard every day, every prayer. I didn't say it first.

"Before they call I will answer; while they are still speaking I will hear." [Isaiah 65:24]

Before we even call. Before we fix our mouths to speak. Jesus emphasized the same point when he was calling Lazarus from the tomb. Read it for yourself.

"Father I thank you that you have heard me. I knew that you always hear me, but I said this for the benefit of the people standing here, that they may believe that you sent me. " [John 11:41,42]

And I grabbed hold of it. I have the Holy Ghost audacity to assume that same assurance since I am an heir of God and joint heir with Jesus Christ. I am dressed in His righteous clothes and stand firmly in the position secured for me by His death and resurrection.

He always hears me. That's settled. It makes worlds of difference. It never has to be discussed again. The Creator of the universe, the one who formed me in my mother's womb, after knowing me intimately, still chooses to hear me always. Not just my words or my songs. He hears me before I even speak. Which makes sense since the Psalmist says He knows every word on my tongue altogether. (Psalm 139:4)

He always hears me. He always hears you. What a wonderful realization! It has to bolster prayer confidence. It diminishes any requirements for fellowship with Him. No special place. No special time. No form. No fashion. He always hears me.

The thing is, expectations make a difference in outcomes.

How disappointed God must be when we pray with no expectation of being heard!

Extensive experimentation on the effect of expectations on outcomes was done by Robert Rosenthal (1964). In one instance, teachers were given D students who to them were labeled as high achievers. That was one group. The control group was the exact opposite.

Wouldn't you know it? The students performed according to the teachers' expectations of them rather than their past and usual performances. Former D students made As and the former A students made Ds. This is my non scientific over simplification of the Pygmalion or Rosenthal effect, but the point is made.

This is one of the reasons mentoring works so well, especially for young people who face overwhelming challenges. It opens the door for a different conversation. The mentor brings a fresh perspective that allows for a change in behavior because of untainted expectations. A person of any age in a behavioral rut finds permission to change and perform according to his or her own aspirations.

So our expectations in our relationship with the Lord are no less important.

Not only should we expect to be heard by the Lord, we should expect to hear from the Lord. It's the way the communication cycle works.

How do we know when we've been heard? It's definitely by the response of the hearer. You know how frustrating it is to say something to someone and they give no indication of having heard you. Not a nod. Not a word. Not a glance. Seriously.

And since we can't see God, what evidence do we have of being heard? First we have the promise which really is enough. But we're sensual people and we like to see and feel.

The hymn that celebrates Mary's adventure "In the Garden" on Easter morning lines out:

He speaks and the sound of his voice is so sweet the birds hush their singing.
And the melody that he gave to me within my heart is ringing.
And he walks with me and he talks with me and he tells me I am his own
And the joy we share as we tarry there, none other has ever known.

So let's look at ways God lets us know we've been heard.

Scripture. We open the bible and read a scripture we've read a thousand times, but this time the words leap from the page as if it is the first time and they speak with such clarity to our present situation.

Let me illustrate this another way.

On July 13, 2013, George Zimmerman was acquitted on the murder charge concerning 17-year-old Trayvon Martin. The young man was returning to his father's house, soda and skittles in hand, in Sanford, Florida, a town that upholds stand your ground laws. Not for everyone, but that's another story. Martin challenged the rent-a-cop's authority; Zimmerman killed him. He never denied it, but said it was in self defense. Local police hid Zimmerman and the incident while they decided how to handle it.

It took 44 days, nationwide media attention and pro-tests with the emerging #JusticeforTrayvon emblazoning the uniform hoodies to force the hand of those who eventually charged Zimmerman with second-degree murder.

Anyway. Acquitted. And I was despondent. I'm old enough to see the rights for which our elders fought being consistently and purposefully legislated away. I was heart sick, being the mother of a son. I was downcast, being a patriot and activist.

And right in the middle of all that – I didn't grab my bible – I heard, in the deepest part of my belly, only three words. And because I'd read them so many times, know the passage well enough to recite along with a reader...I had fainted.

And the words resonating from my belly brought with them a sanctified relief and renewed sense of knowing God still has it all in His hands. I didn't even have to hear the rest. I knew the rest. And therefore I did believe to see the goodness of the Lord in the land of the living. (Psalm 27:13) Not on the other side but on this side of eternity. I didn't have to faint. I could stand on His faithfulness and shine as a sign of the kingdom.

<u>Sermons</u>. We hear a sermon — in person, on television or online — and the preacher preaches as if he or she had been in our prayer room that morning taking notes from both sides of the prayer wheel. Answers every question. Addresses every concern.

Media. The Lord speaks to us in as many ways as necessary for us to get His message. Art. Music. Spoken Word. Dance. Even hashtags. #YesGodIsReal

Signs. Another way to receive clarity of direction from the Lord is to ask for confirmation of His word for us. Gideon asked God for a fleece before he moved on what the Lord had told him to do. (Judges 6:11) I love this story. When the Lord spoke to Gideon, calling him a mighty warrior, Gideon responded, "Who me?" Wonderful. But the Lord didn't seem hesitant or offended at the request for a sign. He simply did as Gideon asked and Gideon obeyed.

One day I asked the Lord for a sign. Actually I'm always asking for signs, but I'll share just one. It was not to confirm that I'd been heard, but that I'd heard His response correctly. So I glibly said, "Let someone give me a brand new bible today. "And then I went about my day without much more thought about it. Later a friend asked me to ride along as she picked up her daughter from college. We rode along talking and laughing about the daughter's day when she handed me a tiny, bright orange New Testament. She said the Shriners had been on campus handing them to as many students as would take them.

It was a good 10 minutes later before the lightning hit me. The fleece. The brand new bible was God's confirmation that I'd heard him correctly. He not only hears us but will confirm our hearing as much as needed. Until we get it.

And don't box God in, requiring Him to speak as He has spoken in the past.

Other people. Sometimes other people bring confirmation without even knowing it. Other times they feel they should share, but with the humility of suggestion rather than instruction. A warning. Beware of Christians bearing words from the Lord that have no seeming relevance to anything in your life. Try the spirit by the spirit.

> *"Beloved, believe not every spirit, but try the spirits whether they are of God: because many false prophets are gone out into the world."*
>
> (I John 4:1)

If you pray, no one else should need to bring something from the Lord that He could easily have told you himself, since you're listening. On the other hand, it is quite comforting to receive the confirmation when the word you've heard causes you to hesitate in receiving it. This is another good reason to be yoked to Christian siblings who are likewise mature in their discipline of prayer and scripture.

Your knower. And then there's that knowing down in the deepest part of our being, without really knowing how we know. We just know. That happened to me very early one Sunday morning when my children were much younger. I'd given permission for my youngest daughter, who was around 14 at the time, to accompany a family friend to her daughter's school, Hampton University. I knew them well so there was no reason for her not to go, except that she would miss church.

When the wake-up call came that morning, I told my friend that my daughter would not be going. I was just as surprised as she was to hear the words come out. I had no logical reason for changing my mind. I hadn't received a word during the night. And I had no explanation for my daughter who thought I'd lost my mind. Try telling a 14-year-old that you changed your mind without having a valid reason.

Can I say I really felt pretty foolish? But I stood my ground. Much later, when our worship service was almost over, we received word that the group had been in an accident. No one was seriously hurt, though each had been injured. This at least gave me some "street cred" and my daughter's looks took on a different tact. They went from, "This chick is crazy," to "This chick is really weird."

I just knew she couldn't go. Maybe having one more person in the car would have changed the outcome in some way that only physics majors can understand. All I knew was that she couldn't go.

To add to the list of how we hear, let's put with regularity. We should hear from God every day. Hearing is a discipline within the discipline of prayer. Faith comes by hearing and hearing by the word of God. Through persistent study of the scriptures we learn to recognize how God speaks and discern that which is outside of God's character. The more we learn, the more God is able to create in us the mind of Christ so that we hear and speak within His will.

<u>Dreams</u> These are near the end of the list because they are not my best tools for hearing. I don't regularly remember my dreams and when I do they don't seem to be messages from the Lord. But this particular one, strange for sure, was just the opposite.

I dreamed I was climbing stairs in my childhood house on Barclay Street, and at the moment I turned from the top of the second floor to continue to the third floor, I heard someone call out to me, "Baby, come here and pray for me." I hesitated but finally peeped into the room. There on the bed was my husband's grandmother, Jessie Johnson, who had never been in that house, reaching for my hand and asking me to pray for her. She was sick and wanted me to pray a healing prayer.

I said, "You want me to pray for you? You should be praying for me." But she insisted and I did as asked. The palm of my hand turned blazing red as if on fire as we prayed.

Maybe eight years later, I was in a situation that took me back to that dream. I went to a prayer meeting at Mother Irene Montgomery's house. If you don't know that name yet, you will before you finish the book. Four of us gathered around her bed and she reached for me, in the same way Granny had in the dream. She said, "Come lay your hands on me. You, come here." Again I demurred. "Me? Pray for you?" Her

"Yes" was enough to give me the confidence I needed and to never ask that question again.

People who are avid dreamers hear from the Lord with great frequency and can expect instruction as well as confirmation through this exchange.

And sometimes we don't know we've heard from the Lord until after the fact.

It was a Tuesday. April 21, 1987. I'd been to 6:30 a.m. prayer at church and shuttled all the kids to school. Since I had a short breather before a doctor's appointment – just a regular checkup – a nap seemed most appropriate.

It was that good kind of sleep that only happens when it's unscheduled and no one else is in the house. Good sleep. But I had to get up by 11.

Suddenly as I drifted on whatever cloud was passing by, there was a loud bang on the front door. The kind of bang that's made by those huge posts police carry to smash in doors. It startled me. But I was not disturbed. Actually I was glad to have been awakened in time to make my appointment.

Everything went fine at the appointment and I returned home to begin afternoon chores before the Mommy taxi went into full speed. When I went into the house nothing caught my attention.

But as I entered the kitchen my eyes fell on the back door. It was open. Not ajar. But fully open. And I hadn't left it open. Not only that. The top of the door was actually missing. I know it was an old house and that everything was a little fragile. But really, the top of the door was gone.

It could have been a scene from one of those old Japanese movies where some monster opens his huge mouth and bites off the top of a door. Or grabs the door with his huge hand and rips off the top. Unbelievable.

So I went upstairs to check. I know I shouldn't have but in that moment fear didn't register. So I went upstairs only to find that whoever had come in helped themselves to everything electronic–televisions, VCRs, radios and whatever gadgets the children may have had then.

Police reports done and aside, I realized that the Lord had gotten me out of that house. The loud knock on the front had been the robbers' way of checking to see if anyone was home. It gave me a way of escape that probably saved my life. One can only conjecture the outcome if drug influenced robbers had come into the house to find me asleep upstairs.

This is just one of the many extraordinary moments of grace that always elicit boundless gratitude for my Father.

And I didn't realize it until after the fact.

God always speaks to us and the more we grow in the relationship, the more we hear what He has to say.

We shouldn't have to wait for heaven to hear God say, "Well done."

We should hear that on some Tuesdays when we've gone out of our way to be kind to some really unkind person, without broadcasting it on Facebook.

We should hear that on some Thursdays when our throw-back is to remember an elder and provide transportation to a doctor's visit.

We should hear that on some Wednesdays when we settle in for some quiet time.

One day I was walking along a strip mall going into the market. I encountered a gentleman whose face was covered with tumors, literally covered. As I composed myself so as not to react badly, I heard the Lord say, "Suppose your soul looked like his face and his soul looked like your face." Really. My first thought had been to pity the gentleman for having to navigate society with such a face. We can be so cruel to each other. But the Lord's words moved me to another thought. How caught up we can be on outward appearance with little regard for what's inside us.

I can't list the number of times I was on deadline at the newspaper and a story fell through or an error was found that could not be corrected in time to run it. Or we found out at the last minute that an ad had been incorrectly scheduled to run. An editor's nightmare. And without a doubt, before I even had a chance to ask for help, a completed piece would show up in my inbox that needed little or no editing and could be inserted just in the nick of time.

Or the times I sat at my desk and shivered – I told you I'm always cold – and thought, "Okay. I'll wrap up and go to the corner to get some soup." And my right hand woman, Wanda Pearson, the voice of the *AFRO American Newspaper* would come into my office and set a cup of soup complete with crackers in front of me. She'd say, "I thought you'd like some hot soup." Love that girl! Love the Lord who always hears my cry.

While we don't have the power to control outcomes — neither should we since God has the big picture — we do get to rest in the assurance that we are always and forever heard whenever we communicate with the Father. And He will always answer even before we speak.

CHAPTER 2:

The Day I Met Jesus

I love those stories of people's lives and how meeting the Lord turned them totally around. I love the ones where people had been gangsters and just when the police were about to arrest them, some angel of the Lord intervened and they avoided jail and hell with one finessed stroke of the Holy Spirit; the stories of the women who didn't know their bodies were the Lord's temples and should be guarded and protected as such; the men who had previously taken out their aggression on everyone who loved them until the Lord overwhelmed them with His own loving presence.

I don't have one of those stories. I didn't have a day. I didn't have an evening. I didn't have a prayer meeting or a Bible study where the Lord met me. I didn't have a mourner's bench experience where the tongues began to proceed after much abuse by the church Mothers. I don't have one and I wish I did.

As a child I knew the Lord and I can't tell you how or why. I wasn't raised by super religious people. In fact, although my grandfather William Henry Scott had been a deacon at Mt. Zion Baptist Church under the leadership of Rev. Walker H. Dawson, he didn't go to church every Sunday. Neither did his wife, my step grandmother Myrtle Greenhill Scott. Somehow, and none of us can figure out how, the task of taking me to church fell to my Uncle Melvin, the 16-year-old usher, who also read the bible to me at night before I went to sleep. I had such an understanding of what he was reading that by four I could read it myself and attempted my first sermon from I John 4.

"How can you say you love God who you haven't seen and yet hate your brother who you see every day. You're a lie and the truth ain't in you." I know. You wish all the sermons you hear are that short. But I preached it over and over again. Don't know why it was that verse that caught my attention. And in my early preaching days an aunt said I always asked them questions about the bible that the adults couldn't answer. I don't remember that part.

I said all of this to lead up to the question, "Are you saved?" It's a question we don't ask as much as we used to. We assume now that if a person is nice or attends church they're probably saved. Saved meaning they've surrendered their lives to the leadership of God through Jesus Christ for Him to become their Savior and Lord.

The most thorough answer I've ever heard, and one that made us laugh when we were children, was, "I'm saved, sanctified, filled with the Holy Ghost, fire baptized and running for my life." The last part signifying that the adversary, the devil was pursuing them to coerce them to sin, so running was required to maintain their saved state. The thing about losing salvation is a topic for another book. Just let me say I believe once saved, always saved. Read John 10:28-29. Once saved. Always saved. Oops. I forgot a phrase. "And I wouldn't take nothing for my journey."

It's important to talk about salvation when we talk about prayer. It's important to know where we stand, where we fit in the family of God. It would be improper to infringe on an inheritance to which we are not entitled. It would be improper to call God our Father unless we mean it and desire to live within His prescribed parameters and thrive according to His plan for our lives.

Are you saved? Have you surrendered your life to the Lord? Do you know what that means? Unless we have full understanding we are likely to block our own prayers with our own misgivings. We are likely to ask with no expectation of receiving. We are likely to ask outside of God's will. We are likely to ask and be crushed when asking produces nothing.

Being saved means we are redeemed by God through the blood of Jesus. We are bought back from a life of sin and brought into the eternal life we are covenanted because of

God's grace. Because of Jesus' supreme sacrifice we are covered and cleansed by the blood He shed on the cross, having taken on our sin as His own. Therefore we walk worthy because we walk in His worthiness. We walk rightly because we walk in His righteousness. We are clothed in the righteous clothes of Jesus Christ and are therefore heirs of God and joint heirs with our elder brother Jesus Christ.

So when we pray, we do so "dressed in His righteousness alone, faultless to stand before the throne."

And when we worship, we recognize the perfect person of God and remind ourselves that we are privy to Him because of His grace.

And when we praise, we invoke His presence because He inhabits the praises of His people.

And when we dance, we do so with gay abandon as David danced, as if no one was watching.

And when we sing, we should "sing lustily and with good courage. Beware of singing as if you were half-dead, or half-asleep; but lift up your voice with strength." [John Wesley]

We are to come as a little child, with a little child's faith, for of such is the kingdom of God.

Being saved is all about God and the lengths He's gone to, to bring each of us back to Himself.

Being saved is simply our consent to be loved beyond anything our hearts can imagine.

Being saved is simply our consent to be forgiven for every sin we've ever committed and every sin we ever will commit.

Being saved is simply our willingness to surrender our own will and allow the Lord to make His will known to us — knowing that everything, every gift, every talent, every skill, that we will ever need has already been given us. All I have needed His hands have provided. Great is God's faithfulness to me.

<u>Our Grace Package</u>

This is my term for the relationship we enter into with the Lord at our recognition of His Lordship in our lives. He's not new to us. He made us. He had communion with us before He formed us in our mother's wombs. We had intimate relationship and foreknowledge of God before we came here.

But we came here. And we lost our memory. And we forgot from whence we'd come. I always pray for my grandchildren to remember heaven. I know it sounds silly, but I do. I think somewhere in their bellies can be recorded the smell of heaven and the atmosphere of heaven and the joy they knew before they left. I think that's the thing that attracts even the hardest heart to newborn babies. They're so soft. So innocent. They smell so different. They seem to draw us in. Many of our hard hearts are operated on as a result of our interaction with babies.

I remember the first time I saw Trenae, my first granddaughter. She was still in the nursery at City Hospital in Baltimore and when I looked at her, hadn't even held her yet, I saw in her what seemed like a broad chested strong woman who would challenge the world and make her own way. I wasn't wrong. She has challenged us every day and continues to do the same in her sphere of influence.

When we become saved with our own consent, we become privy to what I call a grace package. We become aware of God's grace that actually has been in operation in our lives from the beginning. Methodists call it prevenient grace. We become aware of God's mercy, which along with God's goodness, follows us all the days of our lives — having our back as we say — protecting us from whatever evil would overtake and destroy us.

In that package is healing, which is the will of the Lord.

In that package is deliverance, which is the will of the Lord.

In that package is joy, that which is of the Lord only, that gives us strength; not to be confused with happiness that is more situational. Even in the midst of a tragedy, a "saved saint" can maintain joy, knowing that God has it all in His hand.

I used the title, The Day I Met Jesus because everyone ought to have such a remembrance. If not a day, then certainly what life was like before meeting Jesus as opposed to life with Jesus. I loved the stories I used to hear in church in what Black Baptists call devotions. Some would read scripture; others would sing a song. Some would pray a prayer.

But all would optimally talk about their life before they met the Lord and after. So much so, that as children, we not only knew their prayers by heart but also their testimonies because they told them so often and almost always the same way. Now that I'm older, I suspect they just enjoyed telling the story and hearing it over and over again. Hearing how the Lord had rescued them as a "brand from the burning." How they'd almost "made hell" as some would say. How they thought they were on the right track but the Lord found them and scooped them up and turned their lives around.

And the inevitable outcome: I looked at my hands and my hands looked new. I looked at my feet and they did too. I started to talk and I had a new talk. I started to walk and I had a new walk.I looked all around me, it looked so fine. I asked the Lord if all were mine. This was the elders' way of saying if any man be in Christ he is a new creature. Old things are passed away. Behold all things are become new. (2 Corinthians 5:17)

It's important to note that salvation is the first day's work; it's only the beginning. The Lord put that work into operation from our inception. He waits for us to catch up and give consent, since we were not made to be puppets.

We have been saved. We are being saved. We shall be saved. Salvation is the ongoing, progressive work of the Lord that has already been done. You are saved and sealed until the Day of Redemption. (Ephesians 4:30)

Comfortability

He comes

He stands

He knocks

He waits

Your door, your house, your hood

He comes

All we have to do is open the door

All. Just open

Not make anything happen

Not produce anything

Not promise anything

Just open the door

Myriad of things to satisfy

Wife. Husband. Children. Friends.

Strings attached

Employers

Jesus just wants you to open the door

Uncomfortable

Remember we're related

Comfortability written on our Holy Ghost DNA

More like Him than we'll acknowledge

People die young, soon, moved into desired mix of divinity and humanity

Divinity has desired room, ration, with humanity

Comfortability

At ease with life and death

No fear of either

Comfortability with eternity

Comfortability with God's control

Stop striving

Rest is what evil doesn't want us to achieve

Oppresses. Presses. Pushes. Opposes.

Push back

With Comfortability

Written August, 2011

CHAPTER 3

Come Boldly

*Let us therefore come boldly unto the throne of grace,
that we may obtain mercy, and find grace to help in
time of need.* [Hebrews 4:16]

Have the audacity to go in, acting as if you belong,
even if you don't feel it. Go in as if the whole
concept was conceived with only you in mind. Because it
was. If you had been the only one on earth Jesus would have
still died on the cross. Just for you.

The Lord dropped these words into my spirit years ago as
I nervously ministered to someone I'd never met before. He
was in the last stages of HIV-AIDS. This was before treatment
was as effective as it is today. In this fairly dark and dreary
room at day's dusk, I sat at his feet and held his hands with no
idea what to say beyond hello. I looked at his coworker, my
friend, who'd asked me to visit. She looked so confident that

I'd know what to do. He'd never been a churched person but had a civilian understanding of the greatest story ever told. This is all I knew about him. And that he was dying.

Out of the vacuum between my heart and mind came these words. "If you'd been the only one on earth." He was as intrigued by these words as I, who was also hearing them for the first time. What a great opening I thought admiringly of the Person who'd spoken it to me. "If you'd been the only one on earth, Jesus would still have died on the cross so you could have eternal life." His eyes opened wider as he leaned in to hear more of this story I was bout to tell. And from that point I had his enrapt attention and surprisingly some pretty good stuff to say until we embraced following his submission of his life to Jesus Christ as his Lord and Savior. He got it and rejoiced in the new belongingness he was experiencing for the very first time. My only regret was that he hadn't heard the story earlier in his life.

He died two days later.

What gets in the way of our coming boldly is not knowing who we are.

Do you know who you are? I mean really. Do you know who you are? I didn't think so.

Most of us don't and we're getting our definitions from the wrong people.

We walk around with our God-blessed selves looking down trodden and defeated.

We walk around with our heads bowed to the troubles of the world rather than stepping as the children of God that we are.

We, too often, accept defeat as a fact of life rather than realizing we have inroads to the King. Jesus said, "*In this world you shall have trials and tribulations but be of good cheer, for I have overcome the world.*" (John 16:33)

And we are likewise over-comers, because we are in Christ. In Him we live, move and have being. (Acts 17:28) In him we exist as new creations. In him we thrive in resurrection life and power.

Simply because.
Don't take my word for it.
I'll take you to the Book.

This is what it says about you, and I'm only looking in the New Testament for now.

Jesus says to the disciples, "You are the salt of the earth." (Matthew 5:13) He says, "You are the light of the world." (Matthew 5:14) As he invites them to accompany him on a short journey of training and indoctrination whereby He will fill them with all He is and has and then, after leaving them, send another Comforter to go with them for the rest of their journeys.

It is the same for us.

Someone compiled this work, "Who I Am in Christ," and did the work for me.

Who I Am In Christ
I Am Accepted...

John 1:12 I am God's child.

John 15:15 As a disciple, I am a friend of Jesus Christ.

Romans 5:1 I have been justified.

1 Corinthians 6:17 I am united with the Lord, and I am one with Him in spirit.

1 Corinthians 6:19-20 I have been bought with a price and I belong to God.

1 Corinthians 12:27 I am a member of Christ's body.

Ephesians 1:3-8 I have been chosen by God and adopted as His child.

Colossians 1:13-14 I have been redeemed and forgiven of all my sins.

Colossians 2:9-10 I am complete in Christ.

46

Hebrews 4:14-16 I have direct access to the throne of grace through Jesus Christ.

I Am Secure...

Romans 8:1-2 I am free from condemnation.

Romans 8:28 I am assured that God works for my good in all circumstances.

Romans 8:31-39 I am free from any condemnation brought against me and I cannot be separated from the love of God.

2 Corinthians 1:21-22 I have been established, anointed and sealed by God.

Colossians 3:1-4 I am hidden with Christ in God.

Philippians 1:6 I am confident that God will complete the good work He started in me.

Philippians 3:20 I am a citizen of heaven.

2 Timothy 1:7 I have not been given a spirit of fear but of power, love and a sound mind.

1 John 5:18   I am born of God and the evil one cannot touch me.

I Am Significant...

John 15:5   I am a branch of Jesus Christ, the true vine, and a channel of His life.

John 15:16   I have been chosen and appointed to bear fruit.

1 Corinthians 3:16   I am God's temple.

2 Corinthians 5:17-21   I am a minister of reconciliation for God.

Ephesians 2:6   I am seated with Jesus Christ in the heavenly realm.

Ephesians 2:10   I am God's workmanship.

Ephesians 3:12   I may approach God with freedom and confidence.

Philippians 4:13   I can do all things through Christ, who strengthens me.

We are because He is and because He is in each of us.

Or didn't you know that Jesus is in you, is the question Paul asked the Corinthians. [2 Corinthians 13:5]

Same question for each of us. Didn't you know? Do you know? Are you waiting for some type of manifestation or are you willing to accept by faith, as you did when you prayed the Sinners' Prayer, that you are now His and nothing and no one can pluck you out of His hands. (John 10:29)

Armed with this knowledge in head and heart, approach the throne of God boldly, knowing you have space and place simply because you are God's child, Jesus' sibling and joint heir. Don't go as a beggar with a laundry list, but as a child with full understanding that heritage is not to be denied and that the Father waits to commune with you always.

Have this imaginary letter in your heart:

Beloved Child,

I've spent most of your time on earth trying to convince you of my love. We didn't have that problem when we were together in heaven before I formed you in your mother's womb. We were great friends and were in constant communication. And I want the same thing with you now.

But it's so hard to get your attention. You keep looking at your scars. I'm looking at your wounds. You keep looking at the marks you bear. I'm looking at the tales they each tell. You keep looking at your sins. And all I see is Jesus. I see the wounds he bore to free you, the stripes he wore to heal you, the blood he shed to deliver you. You look at your apparel. I look at the righteousness in which you're clothed.

And all I see is Jesus. I see the love he has for you. I hear the prayers he prays for you. I see the Comforter he left for you. You look at your lack and I see the inheritance you have as a joint heir with Him. I have loved you with an everlasting love and have established you in my love.

Don't look down. It diminishes you. Don't look back. It distracts you. Don't look east or west. It slows you down. Look to me. Look up. I love to see your face because when I look at you, all I see is Jesus.

Your Heavenly Father

Go with assurance of the relationship that allows for transparency and pure honesty.

Go with the assurance that God is not only present for you but also for others you'd bring along.

I enjoy the father stories because my earthly father was not present in my life. It tickles me down deep to know that God is my Father and joys in our relationship. I feel like the little kid who has a great big secret but can't keep it secret because it's too good.

One of my early confident moments came on the cusp of an out of town worship experience that required expenses some of the choir members couldn't cover. Some came to me with concern, especially one older couple that was fairly new to the church and to the faith.

Imagine my surprise when I confidently told them not to worry and asked them whether or not they really wanted to go. When they responded that they did, I said, then God is going to do it for you because I'm going to ask Him. Seriously? Where did that come from? Such bravado. Really? So I quickly kneeled to pray for them in my favorite corner by the baby grand piano I loved so much. The church bought it for me to play in worship. A digression. I apologize.

Anyway we prayed. And the next time I saw them they were bubbling over because, you guessed it, they now had the money they needed to pay for transportation and expenses. They were over joyed and had learned a great lesson in praying boldly, not just in asking for things, but in praying for others.

I was relieved and overjoyed. But I was also tickled because I didn't have my money yet.

But we all went and had a wonderful time of worship.

In a similar situation, the leaders of the church were planning a retreat in Oklahoma and the project manager had put us on a payment plan. Each time she'd ask for my payment, I'd say to her, "I don't have it, but I'm going." Each time she'd sort of shake her head in wonderment and walk away. This continued for about eight weeks, until the day the final payment came due and I gave her the same spiel on the telephone. "I don't have it, but I'm going."

She challenged me, reminding me that it was the very last day and she would be picking up tickets for those who'd paid in full. My response was as always. "I don't have it, but I'm going."

About an hour after our conversation, my phone rang and I heard the excitement in her voice. When she'd arrived at the travel agent's office and looked at the printed list of travelers, the first name on the list was mine and it was marked, Paid in Full. That has been at least 33 years ago and to this day I don't know who paid for my trip. It was a God-blessed experience for all of us and the project manager had her socks blessed off by my story.

I love that feeling of telling people my Father will do it because I ask Him to. Many people have that with their earthly fathers and know exactly what I mean. When another child is being deprived of something you might ask your father to provide it with permission of the parents.

When another child is in danger you might run to your father for protection in that moment. It's the same kind of feeling. It's not to demote God to a bell hop, but it's that confident knowing of a child with a good father has — that he will always do what is best, always provide protection, always delight in the child's company.

I watch my son-in-love, Jamal, when his children come around. His whole countenance changes. His cheesy grin wraps twice around his face, as he says, "My babies." Even when shown an old photo, "Look at my babies."

That's the inner warmth I get when I'm in the presence of the Lord. That's the warmth that overtakes me sometimes when my mind is a million miles away and involved in something far afield. Suddenly, it's as if a ball of heat begins to generate from the depth of my being. And in that instant I'm reminded of the great love God has for me and that I'm His forever. Remember.

Let us come boldly unto the throne of grace, that we may obtain mercy and find grace to help in time of need. Hebrews 4:16

We have standing in the throne room. We have standing in God's holy hill.

And so, as children, we can ask without reservation, asking within the will of God, asking under the instruction of the Holy Spirit. Knowing that God is not just able, but willing to perfect those things that concern us.

Ask, giving assent for God to move, breathe, stop, start, heal, deliver, set free, detain, arrest...whatever you bind on earth shall be bound in heaven. Whatever you loose on earth shall be loosed in heaven.

Whatever it is comes under the unspoken contract of the genius of prayer.

Amen!

Chapter 4.

Prayer Without Ceasing

*W*e are encouraged through the scriptures to be enduring in our prayer. Jesus told the parable in Luke 18:1 that taught men should always pray, and not faint. Not give up on God being faithful to be and do as He said.

I Thessalonians 5:17 also emphasizes the need to be constant and pray without ceasing.

The always seems to be the constant and the point is made that as our relationship matures, our faith deepens and we can expect ongoing outcomes that speak to the character of God.

What we are not limited to is choosing how we will pray. As always we have options that meet our needs on any given occasion.

If you allow the Lord to turn your whole body into a prayer instrument then you never have to stop being part of the steady stream that works its way to heaven constantly.

If you pray with your mouth you can let the words flow.

If you pray with your hands you can clap your timber.

If you pray with your feet you can dance your way through.

If you pray with your jewelry you can fill the air with the beauty of praise.

Wait. Pray with jewelry. What?

Well, why not.

I have earrings that are adorned with the Gye Nyame of Ghana that denotes "except God," in the same way as the Psalm:

> *Except the Lord build the house, they that build it labor in vain.* [Psalm 127:1]

Don't you know I wear those earrings when I need the Lord to perfect something that concerns me? Don't you think I put them on to remind myself I'm in prayer posture sending up and out prayer power that moves the enemy away with his attacking imps; that sends out the word of God that will accomplish all He sends it to do?

Absolutely.

Methods

We can pray aloud, speaking as if God is a visible person in the room – always with the expectation that He will answer in His own way. We can sit in silence and allow the Lord to work out the prayer inside us. We can pray in our native language – not necessarily just asking for things – being guided by the Holy Spirit.

Or we can pray in our prayer language, for those who have received it or require it. This is always a point of conversation as not every Christian is invested in or sees a need for a prayer language.

This is different from the gift of tongues that is given only to some Christians, as is every other gift. This is a heavenly language that seems to heighten our communication as it bypasses the thoughts and distractions we battle when we pray with our own understanding. It's as if the Spirit Himself gives life to our tongues to speak sounds we've never heard, that make no sense to our minds. It can be a relief from the strain of putting words to our desires and it can be a help as we are lifted above our understanding.

We can also pray, praise and worship using the actual words of scripture.

*I will enter your gates with thanksgiving in my heart
and into your courts with praise.
I'm thankful unto you and I bless your name.
For you are good; your mercy is everlasting and your
truth endures to all generations.*

[Psalm 100:4,5]

I will bless you Lord at all times; your praise shall
continually be in my mouth
My soul shall maker her boast in you Lord; the humble
shall hear of it and be glad.

[Psalm 34:1,2]

I love the command to put the Lord in remembrance of His word, and I'm sure I've used it more than most. I can get down with some, "You said...." Remember, "You said..." I used to feel like a subordinate teenager when I first started but after many years of practice I wear it well and often.

One of my favorites:

I have set watchmen upon thy walls, O Jerusalem,
which shall never hold their peace day nor night, you
that make mention of the Lord, keep not silence,
And give Him no rest until he establishes Jerusalem
and makes it a praise in the earth.

[Isaiah 62:6,7]

How wonderful this is! Our job is to make mention of the Lord – to cry our day and night and proclaim Him to Lord of Lords and King of Kings – to let the world know who He is. Oh, and by the way, whatever your particular assignment is – give God no rest until it is done.

So I've prayed over the years – I will give you no rest until you establish Baltimore and make it a praise in the earth.

58

And I'm not deterred by the events of April 2015 – uprising and all. That was one of the best things to ever happen. It unearthed the injustice that residents had been screaming about for years.

And the conversation changed. Local hospitals began creating real entry jobs with starting salaries that can actually support families. And new centers opened to keep children safe after school and on weekends when they are most in danger. People who never talked to each other started talking. And "everybody and his mother"ran for political office the next year, making for a fairly new city council. It doesn't always look like the answer when it erupts, but sometimes it is. It may not always look like deliverance but sometimes it is.

Posture

Let's talk about posture in prayer. Again, it is our choice as we are led by the Spirit. And please don't be afraid of falling asleep. If you do, you probably need the rest. If you do, that does not deter the Lord from His part in the prayer process. Remember Abraham was sound asleep when the Lord sealed the covenant with him. He didn't need Abraham's conscious participation. (Genesis 15:12) Our biggest role is to show up in love and spend time with the Lord.

Sitting.
Standing.
Kneeling.

Walking.

Dancing.

Lying prostrate. This is one of my favorites. It's my "go-to" when I feel out of sorts and off balance. Sometimes my body is sick. Sometimes when my heart is sick. Sometimes when I have no idea what is wrong. Or at times when my behavior has disappointed me.

I lay myself down on the floor, face cradled in my arms. I'll cover myself with a blanket – I'm always cold when the rest of the world is comfortable. And I have many blankets, but I'll talk about them in the next chapter.

I'll give God permission to bless me – operate on me, re-work me, fix something, set something free, heal something – in whatever way he sees fit. When I'm in that place I have no idea what's going on inside but I know he does, and I can trust him to do whatever is next in line to be done.

I give God permission because he doesn't violate the free will he's given me. If I'm determined to hold a grudge against someone, he'll let me do it. He'll let me do it until I realize that it's only making me sick and not in the least bit affecting anyone else. And it's at that point that I'll lay myself down.

I give God permission because it's a sign of my acknowledgement that only God can work the good work he's begun in me – only God knows what it is and how it should be done.

Intercession

We all know we should pray for others but sometimes it gets lost in our lives. We're good for a one-time application but what about the ongoing.

We are encouraged to pray for world leaders, national and local leaders. We are encouraged to pray for political leaders, spiritual leaders. We are encouraged to pray for our pastors and teachers and all who labor in the word. Added to the list are our family members and friends, the church members and visitors, the community members and those who come and go.

But should we call all those names every time we pray? Wouldn't be practical. Would surely slow the flow. Would postpone getting to the new stuff.

The priests in the Hebrew Scriptures had the right idea. They wore breastplates over their hearts. On these plates were graven the names of the tribes. Now these were the chief priests who only entered the temple once a year. But when they entered the presence of the Lord, the names of the tribal heads were with them, and received the benefit of God's presence. (Exodus 28)

I adapted this to my own situation some years ago. One of my daughters brought a tee shirt from her vacation in Myrtle Beach. Okay, full disclosure. I'm five feet tall. Have been since I was 10 years old. Get it out. Get over it. So this long sleeved tee shirt fit me like a dress. But the benefit of it was that when the idea hit me, there was room enough and some to spare to write the names of everyone I knew on this shirt.

And when I went into prayer, I'd just put this shirt on and remind God that I hadn't come alone and to please bless all the members of my tribe, all the ones I bore in my heart. And when I look at that shirt now – I see members who've gone on to glory. My mother. My baby sister. I see members who've grown up and are a testimony to the wonder of God. My children. My mentees. I see tribal members who've grown up to become tribal leaders who have "shirts" of their own.

And I'm always blessed when I take time to pray for someone else to be blessed, with full assurance that God has my back and that my every need has already been supplied because of God's great faithfulness to me. Don't make me shout up in here because I'm on the verge!

But let me say, it's more than just calling out names on that proverbial laundry list. Intercession is standing in the gap – where space exists for evil to invade – to complete the hedge of protection we all require for safety. [Ezekiel 22:30]

When I intercede, I'm standing in my position in the family of God, asking God to show himself strong on behalf of someone else, in the same way he shows himself strong for me.

In the same way. With the same vigor. With the same mercy. With the same grace. With the same intention.

A story if you please.

Finances weren't easy for this 40-year-old seminary student until I received scholarship funds for the Urban Ministry program I was in at Wesley Theological Seminary. I loved this school. I have to tell you that I even rejoiced when I read the catalog and knew from that point that it was exactly the right place for me.

During the more difficult days, I was summoned to the dean of students' office for consultation. My tuition was behind. I was attending classes although I really wasn't allowed during this time. The dean asked a few questions about my situation and suggested that perhaps this wasn't the right time for me to be in school. It was that question that sparked a passionate reply that grabbed the dean's attention. If there was anything I was sure of that day, it was that I was in exactly the right place at the right time. It was exactly what God had ordained for me for that season of my life. And I knew it because of the breath of new life I was enjoying since I'd enrolled and begun classes.

One of the things I loved about Wesley was its instructors. Some of them were quite intellectual and full of information. They weren't the touchy feely kind who made you want to spend time with them over meals. Some of them were so well traveled and well read that they were a touch foreboding – great teachers nevertheless.

What I loved about them, young and old, was that eventually you would meet Jesus in each of them. What that means for a Black Baptist is that at some point their tenderness for their Savior became evident in the middle of a lesson, without warning and with infectious joy. And that was always a glorious moment.

The dean said to me, once we found common ground, "I'll go with you to talk to [the financial director]," and I put on my big girl pants and said I could do it on my own. The goal was to arrange payments I could actually make. She stood a little taller as she said to me, "But if I go and speak to him, it'll make a difference." That has stayed with me for more than 20 years.

If I go...If I ask...it should make a difference. And that kind of confidence should rest in each of our hearts. That it will make a difference if I ask because of my relationship with the Lord. You know how little kids do it. "You want me to ask my Daddy to get you the ice cream? He'll do it!"

"My Daddy will do it. My Daddy will take you. My Daddy will protect you."

Isn't that the spirit of a child? Isn't that why we're told to come to the kingdom of God as little children?

Anyway, we went to the office of the financial director and the dean merely stood in the doorway. She said, "I'm bringing Rev. Dorothy Boulware to you. Perhaps you two can work something out that will bring her into good standing with the school."

And she left.

And he asked if I could possibly pay $20 a month until the arrears were caught up.

Are you kidding me? All day long I can pay it! And all was well. And all remains well until today especially because of the lesson I learned and continue to share with others.

CHAPTER 5.

A Place of Prayer

*W*hen my neighbor invited me to join her in prayer at her church down the street, she was appalled that I didn't know to bring a blanket and even a small pillow. I was appalled that she was appalled. I'd never been to a church that wanted me to "bed down" for prayer. But then I'd never been to Prayer House of Our Father, founded by Mother Irene Montgomery, a powerful prophet who was then in her late 70s.

When Mother Montgomery and her crew came to pray they meant business, so they came equipped for the battle, whatever it might require. They didn't think prayer was complete without tears, so weeping was one of their prayer tools. The blankets helped them endure – gave them a cushioned kneeling place and a covering when lying prostrate was indicated.

And when they prayed, the place was shaken and prayers were answered.

This may have been the beginning of prayer blankets for me. And today they're a family tradition. I have to say that I'm the person with no blood, or so I'm teased, because I'm always cold. Summer or winter, when everyone else is comfortable, I'm cold. So blankets are my first line of defense when sweaters and jackets won't suffice. I have them scattered around. I travel with a blanket.

And when one of my children was leaving home for school or travel, she requested the blanket she knew I'd been using in prayer. Thus the tradition was born. Now every new baby gets a prayer blanket from Grandma. At every new beginning, there's a blanket from Grandma – one that has been purchased and used for a period of time – specific to the recipient.

Actually, any of my blankets that are tasked to keep me warm, have also wrapped me as I talked to the Lord and listened for his response. I feel secure as well as warm. I think, for me, the blanket wraps me as I imagine being wrapped in the arms of the Lord. And it signals to me that we are enrapt in fellowship and communion.

So whenever I'm wrapped in a blanket I'm in my special place with the Lord.

My special place.

We've talked about praying any and everywhere. We know we can and place is never a deterrent to being heard of the Lord or hearing from the Lord.

But all of us like to have a special place. Guys like the man caves. Women like she-rooms or dens. We like to have a place to sew. A place to exercise. A place for play. A place for sleep. And how we can decorate and equip the kitchen, the place for family meals and daily communion.

Well what about a place for prayer?

Some are lucky enough to have an actual prayer closet to which they can retreat from the world and the family to spend time with the Lord. Some might have an entire room that doesn't have to be occupied by anyone.

Even a special chair in a designated corner is enough.

It becomes a draw to prayer, especially if it has the blanket that's just the right color, and the perfect texture. It draws us to prayer every chance we get.

And if you're a candle person, again, the fragrance of your choice, with a lighter handy for each prayer occasion.

And if you love art, that special piece that calms your spirit or excites your heart.

What about a photo of the grandfather who taught you to pray?

Or some music – Darryl Coley. Vicky Yohe. Fred Hammond. Lalah Hathaway. The Gospel According to Jazz by Kirk Whalum. Take Me to the King by Tamela Mann. Worth by Anthony Brown and group therAPy. Intentional by Travis Greene. Just a few from my playlists.

Whatever music soothes your soul and prepares you to enter into God's throne room.

And in this room, your favorite bible, your favorite version
And in this room, elements for communion, if this is your choice.

When my friend Rev. Barbara Whipple talks about her "time with the Lord," she makes you jealous and raises suspicion that she has something with the Lord that you might not have. She's a serious prayer warrior and devotes one entire day each week to fasting and communion with the Lord. And she doesn't let anything or anyone interfere with that schedule.

That's the kind of dedication that makes for good thriving relationships and that's what we're all looking for.

This special place is for you and the Lord and it's not to be shared with family members or anyone else. If it's just a corner in a room, it might be used at other times. But when you're in there, everyone should know to steer clear.

Susan Frances Booze Byrd Fuller was my grandmother and began every day, except Sunday, in the chair in the left corner of the living room in front of the amazingly huge window that opened out onto Barclay Street in East Baltimore. She'd situate herself there in that large stuffed chair, its arms adorned with doilies either she or her sister, Hattie, had crocheted, fully equipped with her Scofield Bible and not much else. And she'd sit until she felt equipped to start her day, each scheduled fully with its own agenda. Monday, washing. Tuesday, ironing. Wednesday, more ironing. Thursday, baking. Friday, cleaning. Saturday, cooking for Sunday.

And while she did have a bible in her room by her bed, and while she did read it whenever the desire struck; it was in this special chair that she consulted the Lord as she began every day and, truth be told, I couldn't wait for her to leave so I could jump into it. It held a mystery for this child. I wondered what was going on in that chair every morning but I knew it was something to be desired. And now I sort of know. At least now I understand the nature of the conversation.

CHAPTER 6

Keep Your Foot

*A*fter admonishing you for five chapters to find comfort in the Lord's presence, let me bring tension to the situation.

> *Keep your foot when you go to the house of God, and be more ready to hear, than to give the sacrifice of fools; for they consider not that they do evil.*
>
> [Ecclesiastes 5:1]

The Message bible says, *"Watch your step when you enter God's house. Enter to learn. That's far better than mindlessly offering a sacrifice, doing more harm than good. Don't shoot off your mouth, or speak before you think. Don't be too quick to tell God what you think he wants to hear. God's in charge, not you – the less you speak, the better." [Ecclesiastes 5:1,2]*

Lay your agenda aside. Present yourself as a present in the Lord's presence. Come as a prayer instrument to be played by the Holy Spirit to give joy to the Lord, strength to yourself and flight to the devil. Allow heaven to order the time of prayer for the greater good of all participants. Come softly, listening for what is called for. Sometimes complete silence. Sometimes song. Dance. Writing. Groaning. Even sleep. But He knows best.

How long is enough? As long as it takes. Long enough that you become like Enoch and don't want to leave.

The saints of old dedicated themselves to lives of sacrifice and deprivation. They bowed on hard surfaces, clothed themselves in hair shirts and denied themselves food for months on end. I grew up reading stories about St. John of the Cross, Teresa of Avila, Ignatius of Loyola. And there was a part of me that wanted to be like them.

Especially those who bore the marks of Jesus Christ –the stigmata-on their bodies.

I know. Weird kid.

When we come into the Lord's presence, we stand on holy ground. Moses was instructed to take off his shoes. At another point he was to hide himself in the cleft of the rock so he could only see the Lord's hinder parts. And my favorite part of this passage is that as the Lord passed by, He was so holy, so great and gracious, He couldn't contain the worship of Himself.

And the Lord passed by before him, and proclaimed,
The Lord, The Lord God, merciful and gracious, long-
suffering, and abundant in goodness and truth,

Keeping mercy for thousands, forgiving iniquity and
transgression and sin, and that will by no means clear
the guilty; visiting the iniquity of the fathers upon the
children, and upon the children's children, unto the
third and to the fourth generation. (Exodus 34:6.7)

And when Moses left God's presence, his face had to be veiled as it reflected so much of God's glory.

I'm concerned that we've lost our awe of God. In our zeal to worship God, we seem to approach Him face to face as if we are on equal turf. We stand, and we do have standing in His presence, but we sometimes forget to kneel and prostrate ourselves before Him. This puts us on an equal footing that does not exist.

My grandchildren and their friends like to use the term awesome. Everything is awesome. Everybody is awesome. They are awesome (My grandchildren really are. I'm just saying). But not everything is awesome.

And if everything is awesome, then nothing is really awesome.

I like to reserve that word for God.

Our God is an awesome God
He reigns from heaven above
With wisdom, power and love
Our God is an awesome God

I believe it's easier for us to submit to the leading of the Holy Spirit as we center on the "otherness" of God and bow at His feet for fellowship.

I love you, Lord, and I lift my voice
To worship you, Oh my soul, rejoice
Take joy, my King, in what you hear
May it be a sweet, sweet sound in your ear.

I exalt you. I exalt you. I exalt you, Oh Lord.
I exalt you. I exalt you. I exalt you, Oh Lord.

I could go on and on with worship lyrics and psalms of praise. But you get it I'm sure.

Focusing on our own agenda, our own laundry list can keep us so earthbound that we miss the opportunity for divine interaction. We offer our prayers. We list our complaints. We lobby for our issues.

And we miss the opportunity to be fed with heavenly manna.

We miss it when the Holy Spirit gives us wisdom on the word of God.

We miss it when the Holy Spirit gives us words of knowledge that enlighten us on our own situations or situations of others.

We miss it as the Lord opens up to us conditions that need focused prayer and/or fasting.

The Lord is great and gracious enough to share the wisdom we have need of. He's gracious enough to fill us with His peace, His joy, His mercy. We just need to be vessels waiting to be filled.

I am the Lord your God, who brought you up out of Egypt. Open wide your mouth and I will fill it with good things. [Psalm 81:10]

Ever been led to pray for something that made no sense at all at the time?

One morning I couldn't resist the urging to pray for Herbie Hancock. The only one I knew by that name was the popular pianist, bandleader and composer and I had no way of knowing what he needed prayer for.

Anyway, I prayed aloud and called his name.

After the prayer gathering ended, the leader thanked me for praying for his friend who was seriously ill, and known to his friends as "Herbie Hancock." Who knew? His friend recovered.

Maybe the musician got a blessing too.

This is precisely what praying in the spirit entails–more so than praying in tongues. It is prayer that is completely directed by the leading of the Holy Spirit. This vital, inspired prayer can only happen as we yield all that we are to the prayer moment to the One who is the Divine Initiator.

CHAPTER 6A

...And Fasting

his kind goes out only by prayer and fasting. That's the part of the process that freaks us out. I knew she was going to talk about fasting. Yes. And fasting. It's an assault on our routine and on our degree of spirituality since most of us make the Linus face, as we clutch our blankets, when the subject is broached. Fasting. I've got to give up something? Really? And what would that be?

For example, people of faith routinely fast for the season of Lent to signify sharing the suffering of Jesus Christ as he approached His crucifixion. It can look like 40 days of no sodas, no desserts, no cigarettes or whatever we're impressed to do. And then right back to it all after it's over. Some people freeze whatever desserts they've sacrificed during that time.

Some churches start each New Year with a Daniel fast for the entire congregation. You'll remember his fast was no pleasant food and mostly vegetables and water. Daniel and his young compadres were taken into captivity and had foisted upon them the diet of their captors. Daniel insisted they be fed "pulse" and that they would flourish. And they did. They were more brilliant. They were more physically strong. And the light of God shone on their faces.

Fasting Is

Fasting literally means to "shut the mouth." Quiet down. Stop talking. Stop eating. Focus on what the Lord is saying and doing. Shut your enterprise down and engage in heaven's enterprise. In a crazily busy world such as ours, with so many things to distract us, we have many options for things to give up.

But what is it that most distracts us from the Lord? That would be the question to ask when seeking instruction for fasting. Ever asked the Lord for a fast? Fasting is certainly easier when it is ordained and orchestrated by the Lord. I had been reading books on fasting and had on many occasions asked the Lord if it were even possible to fast for long periods of time. Like 21 days. I wanted to do it. The Lord surely must have put that desire in my heart when I wasn't looking.

I'm one of the great lovers of food. At the time I was a church staff member and Bible study teacher at my home church and it was our practice to fast on Mondays until Bible study. That particular Monday it had been difficult. It's important to prepare for fasting. The elimination of sugar and caffeine the day before, replaced by tons of water, protects against the raging detox headache that shows up when you're trying to fast.

So I dragged my gigantic headache to Bible study, and at the end of devotions when we were heading off to our individual classrooms, I heard the Lord say, "Now do the other 20 days." Oh God. I said,"Seriously?" But I did and by the third day, I was okay. I literally felt something like a shimmery drop cloth fall over me. It felt like the covering I needed to be protected during the fast. So 21 days on juice and water. I was good until our entire staff was at lunch at a Piccadilly's in Virginia. I opted for iced tea. The mistake was putting artificial sweetener in it. I thought I was going to die the next day. Other than that it was pretty uneventful. But a wonderful experience.

Types of Fasts

<u>Absolute</u>. This is a total fast from everything, food and drink. Although no health care professional would condone abstaining from water for any length of time, in the bible, Jesus, Moses and Elijah survived 40 day fasts with absolutely nothing by mouth. I think today an absolute fast would mean abstinence from food but certainly having enough water to remain hydrated.

<u>Partial</u>. Taking in certain foods, water, etc. You might consider a period of time without meat. Or without bread. I mentioned the Daniel fast earlier where he partook of no pleasant

food. Many churches adopt this during the first month of the year for a cleansing new start for the congregation. This is a worthwhile project since so much of what we eat is filled with chemicals, preservatives and fillers – most of which are improperly labeled or not labeled at all.

<u>Consecration</u>. This usually refers to fasts that last for part of the day and for a specific length of time, as indicated by the ministry that declares it. For instance, no food until after six in the evening, and then the basics for survival. A balanced meal with no frills and no dessert. During this time only water and/or herbal tea with no sweeteners are taken.

Things to Give Up

We can choose to abstain from foods we need to detox from anyway. Cigarettes to find that we really can live without them. Whatever social media we're addicted to. The time that thing is attached to our ears. I'm old and hate talking on the phone. I love texting or in person conversations. This is also very personal. What distracts me probably wouldn't catch your attention at all. That's why we need instruction.

Instead of giving up something, what about taking on something? Eating healthy food. Walking. Praise dancing. Reading scripture or a particular book. Doing acts of kindness. With anonymity.

These give us a change of focus and lift our eyes and hearts to the Lord, if for no other reason than to keep us on point for the length of the fast. We don't fast to get God's attention. We always have His attention. We fast to gather our own focus on whatever it is the Lord suggests.

Importance of Secrecy

The scripture says don't be bragging to your friends that you're fasting, looking all haggard with your face drawn and your hair all over your head. Don't be sighing like you're about to faint from hunger as you with great sanctity announce to everyone who'll hear it, "I'm on a fast." (Matthew 6:18)

It's like announcing you've done a good deed. Something is lost in the translation if everyone is patting you on the back for doing what you ought to do anyway.

Keep it between you and the Lord, except for those who absolutely need to know, those who are fasting with you or are lending prayer support for you.

The Fasted Life

The fasted life is, as implied, the choice to avoid certain things for a lifetime. It is comparable to the vegan who goes to the extreme of not wearing clothes or using accessories made of animal skins. That's a conscious choice made based on ethical and spiritual beliefs.

One can choose to fast those items that threaten the health. One can choose to eat enough for healthy survival rather than indulge for pleasure. One can choose to fast one meal a day forever. These choices would not be influenced by any corporate fasts called by one's church. They are strictly personal or household decisions.

The first and last words are the same. In all this, be led by the Holy Spirit down to the least detail. When to start and finish, what to fast and the reason for the fast. And then rest in the Lord and allow Him to carry you through with great victory and expect to see the desired outcome because He has foreordained it in His will.

Chapter 7.

Chill. Make yourself
'at home' in God's love.

*T*hat's right. The last word is "chill." And I had to
go to an urban dictionary for the meaning I wanted.
The more mainstream ones referred to the verb and the noun.

To calm down. To hang out. To be easy going. These are
the right ones.

Some would say, "Let go and let God."

And to add to this, while being "chill,"(yes,it can be used
as an adjective too) make yourself "at home" in God's love.

Who would be arrogant enough to talk about being "at
home" in God's love? Extreme intimacy is implied, but the
phrase isn't mine. I found it in *The Message* bible written
by Eugene Peterson, a retired pastor with particular courage,
informed insight and an unusual heart for God.

It has been my pleasure to read this version since I
received the New Testament as a gift from my best friend

more than 20 years ago. After that time, we anxiously awaited each new installment, book by book, until the entire bible was completed. This is undoubtedly my favorite line of his interpretation and I've prayed over it, mused on it and taught it for as long as I've known it existed. So first I want to thank Rev. Peterson for the gift and invite you to read it if you haven't.

At home. The phrase implies something we don't always associate with our Heavenly Father. We stand in awe of Him, in full knowledge that we are dust and He is "other" than we are. We wrestle with being made a little lower than the angels, or God Himself and the temptation to see ourselves as wretches undone or maybe somewhat done.

And yet, when Dr. Peterson read John 15:9, that in the KJV reads: As the Father hath loved me, so have I loved you; continue ye in my love, he heard:

I've loved you the way my Father has loved me. Make yourselves at home in my love.

It's certainly different and it catches one's attention.

At home in my love. So many things come to mind. At home. When you come home you settle in. You take off the world and all that it requires of you. Shoes. Hats. Coats. Professional clothes. Spanx. Bras. And I'll stop right there.

You take off professional behavior, including jargon. You speak to yourself and your family members with cozy language that is easily understood. Ebonics. Slang. Colloquialisms.

How on earth does any of this translate to our relationship with the Lord?

The other thing about being "at home" is that it implies a lack of suspicion of the love motive and of its reaches. Scripture tells us this love has no boundaries, no top, no bottom, no sides, no end.

It's no ordinary love. It's not like any other love we've ever experienced.

It's a love that's determined to love us for no reason other than that God chooses to love us.

It's a love we can't diminish or increase because it's not circumstantial.

It's a love that is targeted toward but rises up within each object of God's affection.

It's redemptive in that it wipes away all past sins.

It's salvific in that it continually makes us brand new.

It's healing in that it quickens our mortal bodies.

It's liberating in that it equips us to choose righteousness instead of sin.

It's overwhelming in that it fills us to overflowing so it can be experienced by those around us.

It's intoxicating in that once we acknowledge and receive it fully, we want everyone else to have the same experience.

Get used to it. Stop trying to deserve it. Stop trying to deny it. Stop trying to qualify for it.

Stop. Linger. Tarry

Make yourself at home in God's love.

And it's intended to be easy.

Really. Easy. That's implied in another of my favorite passages, Matthew 11:28-30, also in The Message. The section is entitled The Unforced Rhythms of Grace. We'll talk about that later.

"Are you tired? Worn out? Burned out on religion? Come to me. Get away with me and you'll recover your life. I'll show you how to take a real rest. Walk with me and work with me – watch how I do it. Learn the unforced rhythms of grace. I won't lay anything heavy or I'll-fitting on you. Keep company with me and you'll learn to live freely and lightly."

How wonderful is this?

If you're alive you're tired. If you're a church member you're at least a little weary. And if you're a leader in a Black church, you're exhausted all the time. Just getting it in for Jesus!

Remember the Sabbath to keep it holy.

Remember when the entire community kept the Sabbath, each in our own way. The Jewish community on Saturday. The Christian community on Sunday. We observed Blue laws. No stores were open. We didn't even have malls then. I know.

The dates are flying over the place. No alcohol or tobacco products were sold.

And not just that.

Sabbath was observed in our households. Anything that looked like work had to be done on Saturday or it couldn't be done until Monday.

We cooked Sunday dinner on Saturday.

We ironed Sunday clothes on Saturday.

We did Sunday hair on Saturday.

We cleaned the house on Saturday so it was Sunday presentable.

And on Sunday the only work that was done was warming the food that had been prepared, and washing dishes after dinner. We spent much of the day in church. The rest we spent in quiet at home reading, talking, snacking.

As a society we have sacrificed Sabbath for success and declared ourselves necessarily productive to "get it in" on all the days. The measure of our success is our perennial activity and our consistently expressed exhaustion.

This was not the plan for Christians. In fact, the Hebrews scripture encourages us to "labor to enter into THAT rest," the "rest" in God that God promises us and facilitates with our permission. [Hebrews 4:11]

So Jesus, in the face of our weariness, invites us to come unto Him and learn of Him to live freely and restfully – to get our lives back from the things that encompass and burden us. The things that distract from our real reasons for being. Walk with me. Work with me. Watch how I do it. Watch me. Walk as I walk. Pray as I pray. Rest as I rest. And as you are beset with life, rely on the Comforter I've sent you to give you guidance and direction.

Ever heard of the Tennessee Walkers? They are champion horses that are trained by linking a young horse with a champ and urging them to walk together so that the gait of the younger is made more sure and correct by the gait of the elder. This is the clearest picture of discipleship I've ever seen. It is exactly what Jesus did with the fishermen he drafted for his contingency. They ate together. They slept together. They fished together. They prayed together. They ministered together.

All the while he was observing their behavior as they were observing His. He was teaching them along the way as they traveled together for three years. Sometimes he was encouraged by their progress. "Flesh and blood has not revealed this unto you," he commended Peter after his declaration that Jesus is indeed the Christ, the Son of the Living God. [Matthew 16:17]

Other times, not so much. "Have I been so long time with you and still you know me not," Jesus chided Phillip in response to his question, "We don't know where you're going, how can we know the way?" [John 14:9]

It's the ups and downs of discipline and is a perfect parenting style as well.

That's why homeschooling is so successful when done correctly. This model makes every minute a teachable moment and it works because it happens within the relationship journey and it sticks because it has relationship markers for memory.

And then there's that thing about the unforced rhythms of grace. I love this phrase so much. It's so simple in its wording, yet so profound in meaning.

Rhythm can't exist without rules. This implies some sort of force to make the rules work.

Music has time rules. It has melodic rules. It has pitch rules. It has all kinds of rules. And there's even a tool called a metronome to help keep rhythm's rules.

This is easily understood. We don't tap our feet quickly to a slow song or dance slowly holding our sweeties when Uptown Funk comes on. It's just not done.

And here we're presented by God with a grace that has no rules, no boundaries, no top, no bottom, no conformity to anything we can understand.

And as this grace has no boundaries, also the rest has no boundaries. It's certainly not confined to a specific day. It invades and pervades every moment of our being. THIS rest, like no other, becomes a part of our fiber and demands we chill in Christ.

And as we are challenged to unlearn the power habits that threaten our existence, we are challenged to learn the unforced rhythms of grace.

Grace has its own nature, its own color, its own multiplicities and it confounds even us who have been saved by it and continue to exist in the family of God because of it. It's a wonder to my soul and such a tremendous gift that I expect we'll be glimpsing God's feet in glory before we have the slightest idea of what it really is.

What I know is this. Once we've really gotten a hint of it…let me change that.

Let me testify a minute. I am a child of God's grace and just the thought of it makes me smile from the depth of my being. It overwhelms me to know how precious I am in the sight of God and that nothing and no one can pluck me out of His heart or His hand.

So rest. I love it. It's a gift. It gives me time and space to become more familiar with myself.

It gives me time and space and hunger to know God more intimately.

It gives me a yearning to allow God more entrance into my life and being.

It gives me a yearning to spend more time just thinking about and talking to and listening to God.

And my friend, this is purely chill time in prayer. Purely chill. Because while I'm still and contemplating, if there are words to be said, I am led to speak them.

If there are songs to be sung, I am led to sing them.

If there are names to be called and request to be made, I am led to make them.

If there are demons to be chased, then worship is summoned from the depths of my being and the room and or the situation is cleansed.

And remember, I don't have to worry about who I am because I am in Him and He made me and knows all about me. He knows me altogether. Altogether. It's a good word we seldom use in this country. Altogether. Every piece of every facet of every aspect of me. And you. After all, He made us. Plotted our paths. Has the whole story from beginning to end. Knows every word we'll speak and every thought we'll have. Altogether. He knows us in a whole way. Altogether. Likewise He's altogether lovely, altogether gracious, altogether lovely, altogether holy, altogether merciful, altogether loving.

By the grace of God.

The last word. Chill. Make yourself at home in God's love.
Learn the unforced rhythms of grace.
By the grace of God.
And be blessed beyond anything you can ever imagine.

My final story. The Day God Showed Up
I know. God shows up every day. But this particular day, my son, a homeless-by-choice young man, was on trial as a victim who had been stabbed repeatedly by a city employee.

Yes he was in jail; had been for 38 days. I always pray for God to bless the son that we share in His own way. And on the day of the trial God showed up in ways we could not even have imagined.

First of all, a young woman attorney helmed the case pro bono. She was well versed and prepared to do her job. We'd never heard of her, but we know her now. She had canvassed the homeless community and found that they know my son and find him likable and helpful. No incidents of violence at all. And in her discourse at the courthouse, she continued to remind everyone involved that the victim had been in jail for 38 days awaiting trial. By the way, this was happening as I was actually writing this last chapter.

The state was unprepared because they assumed this homeless man would come without representation so, having now met the totally prepared attorney, they asked for a continuance. But she said, "No," adding that they were fully prepared to proceed. She had also collected donations to help my son get the basics he needed when he was released –things that get lost when a homeless person goes to jail. And she continued to demand his release by 5 p.m. That day.

The homeless man, my son, had the better representation of the two parties. Oh and did I say he also had a witness who saw him on the ground being stabbed repeatedly by the city employee. Being stabbed, not stabbing.

I would not have known to pray for such a great attorney. A well-prepared public defender would have sufficed. I could not have guessed that a credible witness existed, one who would have come forth. I could not have imagined that the state would not have bothered to prepare a case. On that day God showed up.

This is why I labor to enter into THAT rest, chill and make myself "at home" in God's love. And I'm learning more every day.

I pray that on this journey you have enjoyed the ongoing invitation of this child who has found a wonderful place in God and wants to share it with everyone.

The message is simply, "I've found joy and I've found it in Jesus. I've found peace and I've found it in Jesus. I've found acceptance and I've found it in Jesus. I've found grace and I've found it in Jesus. If you haven't found your own, come share mine."

Peace be unto you and unto yours.

Addendum

These are the saints who had direct and indirect influence on my prayer journey and I couldn't write this book without remembering each of them. I'm sure you'll see them in future books in more detail but their names kept rising up in my spirit as I wrote this one and the only way to include them in such a limited space was to make a list. The names are in chronological order to assist in my senior memory. I hope this will encourage you to write one of your own, giving thanks for the saints who have done their work, and some of them gone on to receive their reward, while making up the great cloud of witnesses cheering us on to our own.

May God be praised for each of them and their solid contribution to my life and the many others they blessed along the way.

Magruder Scott Cockrell
William Henry Scott

Myrtle Jane Greenhill Scott

Gertie Scott Blunt

Melvin Roosevelt Scott

Hazel Martin

Rev. James Garrett

Rev. Walker H. Dawson

Susan Frances Booze Fuller

Charlotte Flowers

Rev. Irvin Charles Lockman

Rida Bell Billups

Victoria Clark

Hattie Childs

Barbara Jenkins Powell

Deacon Melvin Norman

Deacon George Graves

Deacon Charles Beatty

Rev. Leslie Dyson

Bettie Crest Durant

Rev. Mark A. Riddix III

Deacon Harvey Johnson

Rev. Harold A. Carter Sr.

Rev. Oral Roberts

Rev. Geraldine James

Rev. Robert Williams

Mother Irene Montgomery

Doris Payton

Shirley

Rev. Barbara Whipple

Rev. Norman Whipple

Rev. Robbin Blackwell

Apostle Stanley Butler

Rev. Felecia Diggs

Rev. Andre Newsome

Rev. Bertha Borum

Rev. Lenora Howze

KEEP WALKING IN PRAYER……. UNTIL YOU CAN'T COME BACK is a soul-stirring offering to the body of Christ reminding us of the value of prayer and calling us back to the blessings inherent in a life-style immersed in prayer.

Dr. Boulware has passionately shared her journey to a life filled with prayer from her early formation until now with compelling examples of the power and worth of prayer as manifested in her own life. For the novice, Dr. Boulware invites them to a prayer life with her simplistic definition of prayer. "Prayer can happen with no action required beyond breathing. Prayer is the ongoing transaction between us and God, mediated or spurred on by the Holy Spirit, with Jesus at the right hand of the Father interceding on our behalf."

The value she has found in prayer is evidenced in her own personal testimony. She reminds us that we pray to a God who hears and answers our prayers. KEEP WALKING IN PRAYER………. UNTIL YOU CAN'T COME BACK encourages us to examine our expectations in prayer. The reader is reminded that "expectations make a difference in outcomes. How disappointed God must be when we pray with no expectation of being heard."

One expectation that we all have is being heard. She points out that "There's nothing much more precious than the feeling of being heard. She goes on to share how her prayer life has impacted her personally and allowed her to go on by the knowledge that God has her back and she has God's ear." She unselfishly desires to have everyone else who desires it to have a similar expectation. One could feel her passion riveting through the ink on the pages. Even a stranger to prayer could feel confident in entrusting their cares and concerns to the"Father." But she cautions those who have not made them their Savior to do so, if they desire positive results. To demonstrate the impact that our relationship with God has on our prayer life,

Boulware offers an analogy of the expectations one can reasonably have when making a request to a stranger and that of making a request of a relative.

How refreshing her perspective on prayer and worship. It challenges us to embrace a paradigm shift from what we are accustomed to engaging in when we participate in corporate worship by bringing a new openness to the whole notion of worshipping without any preconceived notions or expectations.

Dr. Boulware introduces terms and phrases like "unforced rhythms of grace" which reach to our very core and unearths in us an innate desire for a closer walk with God and a more consistent and meaningful prayer life. Her PERSONAL example of the power of that kind of life as demonstrated on the day of her son's trial offers hope to every hurting parent, every family member or loved one who has been at their wits end needs and will forever belong to my personal vocabulary. The impact of her personal testimonies have left a lasting impression on my life.

Lastly but not least of all, she suggests that we "Lay our personal agendas aside, present ourselves as a present in the Lord's presence. Come as a prayer instrument to be played by the Holy Spirit to give joy to the Lord, strength to yourself and flight to the devil. Allow heaven to order the time of prayer for the greater good of all participants. Come softly, listening for what is called for. Sometimes complete silence. Sometimes song. Dance. Writing. Groaning. Even sleep. But realize that He knows best." The image of being a "prayer instrument" who sings, dances and groans is one that is music to my ears. HOW POETIC!!! HOW SOBERING!!! HOW COMPELLING!!!

This book is an easy read. It's perfect for small group Bible Study or Discipleship Training on Prayer. After reading KEEP WALKING IN PRAYER.......... UNTIL YOU CAN'T COME BACK, one is compelled and persuaded to enhance their prayer life and see the power of God transform their future.

Rev. Dr. Leah White
Pastor of Greater Faith Baptist Church
Baltimore, Maryland
Founder and Ministry Leader of Sisters in Ministry

CPSIA information can be obtained
at www.ICGtesting.com
Printed in the USA
LVOW08s1550070217
523493LV00001B/188/P

9 781498 474542